IMAGES
of Aviation

AUSTER

With its 130hp de Havilland Gypsy Major engine at full throttle a Taylorcraft Auster AOP Mk III ascends rapidly from Rearsby in 1943. Using the first stage of the flap setting produced a take-off run of seventy yards.

IMAGES
of Aviation

AUSTER

Compiled by
Ken Wixey

TEMPUS

First published 1999
Copyright © Ken Wixey, 1999

Tempus Publishing Limited
The Mill, Brimscombe Port,
Stroud, Gloucestershire, GL5 2QG

ISBN 0 7524 1607 3

Typesetting and origination by
Tempus Publishing Limited
Printed in Great Britain by
Midway Clark Printing, Wiltshire

An Auster J/5A with the experimental, Italian 'Bon Martini' four-wheel bogie landing gear, fitted with a caterpillar tyre. This was designed for take-off from undulating ground but was abandoned.

Contents

Acknowledgements

The author is extremely grateful to Brian Pickering of Military Aircraft Photographs (MAP), to Brian Stainer of Aviation Photo News (APN) and to Roger P. Wasley for permission to use their photographs in this book. Thanks also to my wife, Jean, for her patience during those times when 'silence was golden'.

Numerous reference works were consulted, especially the following: *History of the Auster Aeroplane* (A.V. Hitchman); *Beagle Aircraft Ltd* (Midland Counties Research Group); *British Civil Aircraft since 1919: Volume 1*, Putnam (A.J. Jackson); *Aircraft of the Royal Air Force since 1918*, Putnam 1988 (Owen Thetford); various articles in *Aeroplane Monthly* and *Wingspan* magazines as well as *Civil Aircraft Recognition 1962* and *Light Plane Recognition 1975* from Ian Allan (both John W.R. Taylor).

A major overhaul of the 180hp Blackburn Cirrus Bombardier that powers Auster AOP 9 XN409 of the AAC.

Introduction

The origins of Auster aircraft were in Alliance, Ohio, USA, where the Taylor Young Airplane Corporation produced their first Taylorcraft Model A in 1937. This high-wing monoplane with enclosed cabin, side-by-side seating, fixed landing gear and 40hp Continental engine proved popular and over 600 were sold. Subsequent variants culminated in the L-2 (US Army YO-57) and a US Army order for a considerable number of L-2A Grasshoppers.

In the UK, A.L. Wykes obtained a licence to build Taylorcraft Model As and Taylorcraft Aeroplanes (England) Ltd was formed at Rearsby, Thurmaston, Leicestershire, in November 1938. Six US-built Model As and one Model B imported into Britain were typical of those to be built at Thurmaston. The first British-built Taylorcraft Plus C, powered by a 55hp Lycoming engine, flew at Rearsby on 3 May 1939. Of twenty-two more that followed, two had a 90hp Cirrus Minor engine, one becoming the Taylorcraft Plus D prototype. A further eight entered RAF service at the outbreak of the Second World War. When the Air Ministry ordered one hundred more new machines they requested a name for the type. 'Auster', the Latin word for a warm southern breeze, was chosen and Taylorcraft Plus Ds became Auster Mk Is.

The onset of the Second World War saw additional premises acquired for Taylorcraft. As well as producing Auster AOPs (Army Observation Planes), components were built for Airspeed Oxfords, Hawker Audaxes, Hurricanes, Spitfires and Albemarles. RAF Tiger Moths, Hurricanes and Typhoons were also repaired. Auster deliveries began in July 1942 with No.651 Squadron being the first to receive Auster Is. Split trailing-edge flaps were fitted later but otherwise Austers changed little during the war. Only two Mk IIs were built due to a shortage of the Lycoming engines with which they were powered. The 470 Auster IIIs built had the 130hp DH Gypsy Major 1 engine. One was converted to a Model H three-seat training glider similar to the US TG-6 which was based on the L-2. Upgraded Lycoming engines were fitted to 254 Auster IVs, which had increased cabin space for an optional third seat. The most prolific variant, the Mk V of 1944, had blind-flying equipment, a message pick-up hook, alternative twin float or ski landing gear, cable-laying equipment and provision for a camera. Some 800 Mk Vs flew as AOPs with nineteen RAF squadrons as well as Canadian and Dutch units.

The Mk V replacement, the AOP 6, had a 145hp DH Gypsy Major 7 engine, longer landing-gear struts, a larger propeller and external non-retractable flaps to improve take-off. In 1946 the company became Auster Aircraft Ltd and by 1949 had built 296 AOP 6s. Further production started in 1952 bringing the total number of AOP 6s built to some 400. The T.7 dual-control trainer was an AOP 6 conversion, seventy-seven being built, while similar alterations to a small number of Model Ks resulted in the T.10.

The AOP 9 made its first flight in March 1954 with a 180hp Blackburn Bombardier, a larger-span wing with a single strut, cantilever landing gear and an improved blister type canopy. This remained the basic RAF/Army Air Corps AOP aircraft until the arrival of helicopters and some AOP 9s went to India and South Africa. A one-off Mk9 development, the B4 ambulance/freighter, was evaluated for military purposes.

The post-war civil Auster, the J/1 Autocrat, had a 100hp Blackburn Cirrus II and a mass-balanced rudder, the J/1A, a fourth seat (later reverting to a standard three) and the J/1N Alpha, a 120hp DH Gipsy Major 1. Only one J/1S was built – with a 140hp Gipsy Major – but an agricultural crop sprayer, the J/1B Aiglet with the 100hp Blackburn Cirrus, sold well, with seventy-two being exported. A strengthened airframe and dorsal fin, a larger rudder, low-pressure tyres and hydraulic brakes were features of the J/1U Workmaster agricultural aircraft, which had an Avco Lycoming engine.

Similar in appearance to the Autocrat but with a 75hp Continental engine were the forty-two two-seat J/2 Arrows. The one-off J/3 Atom emerged with a Continental A65 engine but, lacking power, was converted to J/4 standard. The J/4 Archer, of which twenty-five were built, accommodated three seats and was powered by a 90hp Cirrus Minor. When the J/5 Aiglet Trainer appeared with shorter wings, it also differed from the J/1B Aiglet in being stressed for aerobatics. Variants were the one-off J/5K with the 155hp Blackburn Cirrus Major 3, the ten J/5Ls, with 145hp DH Gipsy Major 10s, the J/5R Alpine, a hybrid with Aiglet Trainer fuselage, Autocrat wings and Aiglet Trainer ailerons, four J/5Q Alpines with 130hp DH Gipsy Majors and the J/8L, a J/5K re-engined with a J/5L power plant.

The four-seat J/5B Autocar tourer appeared in 1949 with a 130hp DH Gipsy Major 1, wing-root fuel tanks and a larger, domed cabin roof. Of eighty Autocars built, fifteen remained in the UK and sixty-five were exported. To provide extra power for tropical conditions, the J/5E had a 155hp Cirrus Major and served as the prototype for the ninety J/5Gs built with Cirrus Major 3s. The sole J/5GL was powered by an Avco Lycoming engine, while the one-off J/5H was a rebuilt J/5B with a Cirrus Major 2. Some twenty-four Auster J/5Ps were built, with 145hp Gipsy Major 10s.

An agricultural crop-spraying aircraft for New Zealand was made by Auster in 1956, the low-wing monoplane B8 Agricola. Only eight were built before financial problems in New Zealand led to cancellation. One British-registered Agricola, G-APFZ, flew with Crop Culture (Aerial) Ltd in 1959. The Auster C6 Atlantic project had an oleo tricycle landing gear, a Continental E-185-10 engine, easy access via wide doors and Autocar wings but was a one-off due to poor market potential.

In October 1960 Auster Aircraft Ltd was absorbed by Beagle Aircraft Ltd and Auster's J/5V, with a 160hp Avco-Lycoming engine, was developed as a prototype for the Beagle-Auster D series. These comprised the D.4/108 two-seater, D.5/160 three-seater and D.6/180 four-seater, all with Avco-Lycoming engines. A number went into the Portuguese Air Force, others being produced as the Beagle A.113 Husky. During the Beagle take-over, thirty Auster 6s were converted to 6A Tugmaster glider tugs and eighteen built as a 6B luxury variant, which became the Beagle A.61 Terrier Mk1. The Terrier Mk2 possessed a wider-span tail-plane, improved flaps, wheel spats, an improved engine and a Fairey-Reed metal propeller. A one-off Terrier 3 was built, with a 160hp Lycoming 0-320-B2B, and an improved Auster airframe by Beagle produced the A.109 Airedale with the 180hp Lycoming 0-360-A1A, tricycle landing gear, swept-back vertical tail surfaces, streamlined wheel spats and restyled interior. Only forty-three Airedales were built.

Determined to re-establish Britain's pre-war light aircraft prominence, Beagle went on to produce the low-wing Pup series 1, 2 and 3, which developed into the Bulldog military trainer. They produced the 206 twin-engined light transport, the larger 206Y, 206Z and 206C production (series 1). The 206S (series II) had turbo-supercharged engines. The RAF ordered twenty Beagle 206s as Basset CC.Mk1 communications aircraft, while civil 206s went to customers in the UK, Spain, Argentina, South Africa, Sudan, Zambia, USA, Nigeria, Brazil and Australia.

Beagle went into receivership in 1970 and development of the Bulldog was taken over by Scottish Aviation Ltd at Prestwick. Bulldogs served with the Central Flying School, the RAF Flying Training School and sixteen University Air Squadrons.

One
Taylorcraft Auster

A US Army Taylorcraft L-2A Grasshopper, the military version of Taylorcraft's Model D, with a 65hp Continental engine, a two-way radio and a rotating rear seat. To improve visibility, the military variant had a wing-root trailing edge cutaway. Initially designated O-57A, the type was classified in the 'L' category in 1942. A total of 476 L-2As were produced, followed by 490 L-2Bs, specially equipped for service with the Field Artillery.

The US Taylorcraft TG-6 three-seat training glider, an L-2 conversion with an extended glazed nose, was very similar to the British conversion of a Model B to the one-off Model H three-seat glider.

Taylorcraft Plus C.2, HH982 (ex-G-AFVA), a direct forerunner of the Auster. It survived the war to become G-AHAE on the civil register.

This Taylorcraft Plus D, RAF W5741 (ex-G-AFZH), survived the war and became G-AFZI.

Sadly, this is the above Plus D, G-AFZI, after crashing and being written off in October 1963.

Restored to its Second World War camouflage scheme is Taylorcraft Auster 1 LB375, powered by a 90hp Blackburn Cirrus Minor.

Taylorcraft built components for the Hawker Audax, like K5133 shown here. It flew with Nos11, 9 and 1 Flying Training Schools and No.3 Reserve School, but was struck off charge (SOC) in November 1941.

Another type for which Taylorcraft produced parts was the Airspeed Oxford. This Mk II (L4576) is in pre-war overall yellow with clear metal cowlings.

Spitfire components were also made at Taylorcraft. This MkVc (AR501/'NN-D') is from No.310 Squadron.

Some of the many sub-contract parts which made up the Armstrong Whitworth Albemarle were produced by Taylorcraft. This Albemarle (V1599) served as a development prototype in around 1942.

Powered by a 130hp DH Gipsy Major 1 engine, this Taylorcraft Auster III (MT 407) later transferred to the Royal Australian Air Force (RAAF).

This Taylorcraft Auster III (NJ916) was transferred to the Royal Netherlands Air Force but in post-war years was restored to the condition seen here.

A frontal close-up of the Gipsy Major engine and propellor on a Taylorcraft Auster III in 1943. For Auster installation the DH Gipsy Major incorporated aluminium cylinder heads and dual fuel pumps. Thus, unlike the de Havilland Tiger Moth that used the same engine, the Auster III did not rely on gravity feed from its wing tank.

An Auster Mk III (R-15) after transferring to the Royal Netherlands Air Force in around 1948-49.

This Auster Mk3 is seen in 1958 with the serial number A11-53 after transferring to the Royal Australian Air Force. During the production of Mk III Austers, fifty-one were offset for Australian delivery and service with the RAAF.

Other Auster IIIs, IVs and Vs were disposed of post-war to various air forces. This Auster (NZ1702), one of six J/5s ordered by the Royal New Zealand Air Force (RNZAF) in 1947, was for use on forestry patrols and army liaison duties. It was later used for training and given the designation T.7.

Many RAF aircraft were repaired by Taylorcraft during the Second World War, including de Havilland Tiger Moths. This one (K4288) is seen in 1938 when with No.18 ERFTS.

More than 360 Hawker Hurricanes underwent repairs at Taylorcraft. This Hurricane IIB, BE485/'AE-W', is seen in 1941-42 with No.402 Squadron, RAF.

Another Hawker type repaired by Taylorcraft was the Typhoon. This is EK176/'JX-K' when serving with the RAF's No.1 Squadron in 1943-44.

Taylorcraft Auster V TJ458, a modified Mk IV with a blind-flying panel and a 130hp Lycoming engine. Appearing in 1944, the Mk V also had a controllable trimming tab on the port elevator (previous models had a separate trimming vane under the tailplanes), while a tailwheel replaced the earlier skid.

A rare shot of Auster V TJ207 fitted with DH Queen Bee floats and engaged in trials at Beaumaris in 1943. The de Havilland Queen Bee was a radio-controlled target drone version of the Tiger Moth for RAF and Royal Navy use as an anti-aircraft gunnery practice aircraft. Fitted with twin floats, the Navy version was catapulted from warships.

The beautifully restored Auster AOP V NJ695/G-AJXV complete with 1944 D-Day invasion stripes.

An Auster AOP V (TJ527/'BD-L') in service with No.227 Operational Conversion Unit (OCU) in the late 1940s.

This Auster V (TW453), fitted with a glider-towing hook, is pictured at the RAF College, Cranwell, in 1950.

Auster 5D G-ALYG (ex-MS968) was one of many military Mk V machines sold on the post-war civil market.

The civil Auster 5 G-AKWS (ex-RT610), powered by a 150hp Lycoming engine and fitted with a dorsal fin.

Two

Auster Aircraft Ltd (Military)

The Auster AOP 6 first appeared in 1945, entering service in 1947. It had a 145hp DH Gipsy Major 7 engine and featured external aerofoil flaps. This camouflaged RAF machine is VX128.

Here, Auster AOP 6 WJ363 is seen in 1965 when serving with No.38 Group's Communication Flight.

Army Air Corps Auster AOP 6 WE565, with the 145hp DH Gipsy Major 7. Note the auxiliary aerofoil flaps extending aft of the wing's trailing edge.

Undergoing trials here at the Marine Aircraft Experimental Establishment (MAEE) at Felixstowe is Auster AOP 6 VF515, converted to seaplane configuration with twin floats.

In its element, Auster Mk 6 TW566/'PF-Y'/'Y' is shown when serving with No.227 OCU in 1946. This version had a moulded windscreen in place of the earlier fabricated flat-front type, wing fuel tanks of 32-gallon capacity and separate aerofoil flaps beneath the wing trailing edges.

Auster T.7 dual-control trainer prototype VF665 of 1947, at the SBAC Show, Farnborough. The engine was a 145hp DH Gipsy Major 7. Note the RAF Handley Page Hastings four-engined transport in background.

The yellow training band is clearly seen on the rear fuselage of this Army Air Corps Auster T.7, WE591/'Y'. This model was designed to allow the instructor and pupil to sit side by side and was fitted with full dual controls.

This Auster T.7 (WE600) was one of two used on the 1955-58 British Trans-Antarctic Expedition. Fitted with skis or floats, they served as reconnaissance aircraft for the teams involved.

Auster AOP 6 and T.7 cockpits were similar in most respects. This numerical key (1-39) refers to Figure 1 here and Figure 2 below depicting cockpit interiors.

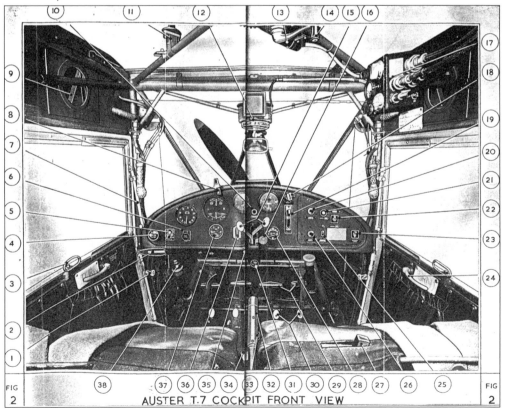

KEY TO FIGURES 1 and 2

1. Port door jettison handle.
2. Parking brake handle.
3. Port window opening catch.
4. Fuel cock control.
5. Ignition switches.
6. Shielded starter button.
7. Port window adjusting stay.
8. Emergency red floodlight.
9. Port fuel tank contents gauge.
10. Fire warning light.
11. Rear view mirror bracket.
12. P.12 magnetic compass.
13. Cabin lamp.
14. Longitudinal trimming control.
15. Throttle lever.
16. Mixture control.
17. Radio control box.
18. Carburettor hot air control.
19. Ground/flight switch.
20. Compass lamp dimmer switch.
21. Identification light morsing button.
22. Identification light switch.
23. Navigation lights switch.
24. Starboard door handle.
25. Emergency lamp switch.
26. Cockpit lamp dimmer switch.
27. Back release for starboard seat (T.7 only).
28. Voltmeter.
29. Starboard rudder pedals (T.7 only).
30. Starboard heel brake pedals (T.7 only).
31. Cabin heat control.
32. Flap lever.
33. Signal pistol stowage (on floor).
34. Hand fire-extinguisher.
35. Throttle friction adjuster.
36. Oil pressure gauge.
37. Oil thermometer.
38. Press-to-transmit button.
39. Ammeter (Mk. 6 only).

FIG 1

AUSTER 6 – INSTRUMENT PANEL

The interior of the Auster T.7 cockpit and forward view; for reference to the numbers see the key above.

FIG 2

AUSTER T.7 COCKPIT FRONT VIEW

FIG 2

25

Auster T.7 NZ1707 in 1964 when with the Royal New Zealand Air Force Auster Flight.

A much-modified Auster T.7 prototype (VF665) after conversion by Marshalls of Cambridge to its M.A.4 form for use in boundary-layer control experiments. A new, square-cut wing of high-aspect ratio with a porous surface was fitted. A small gas turbine in the rear fuselage provided suction for the wing perforations. First flown in 1959, this aircraft crashed on 8 March 1966 and was written off. Note the revised fin and rudder and the stronger landing gear.

Originally an AOP 6, this is Auster WJ401 after conversion to T.10 configuration. It is seen here in 1965 when with the Army Air Corps (AAC) No.38 Communication Flight.

Another Auster T.10 from AAC No.38 Group Communication Flight, WJ363 in camouflage finish.

Designed purely for military use, the Auster AOP 9 was powered by a 180hp Blackburn Cirrus Bombardier, had an increased wing area and was very versatile in its range of duties. The prototype, WZ662, seen here, first flew on 19th March 1954.

Undergoing carrier-deck landing trials in the 1950s aboard HMS *Hermes*, Auster AOP 9 WZ721 of the AAC is about to touch down. This exercise was intended to enhance closer cooperation between land and naval forces. The AOP 9, with its robust landing gear, was potentially a good candidate for carrier operations.

A nice aerial shot of Auster AOP 9 XR244 of the Army Air Corps Historic Flight, in around 1982.

At a late 1950s air show, AAC Auster AOP 9 WZ716 stands beside Royal Navy Hawker (AWA) Sea Hawk FB.3 WF295, with its wings in folded position. The noteworthy features of the AOP 9 are evident – a superb all-round view, balloon tyres, deceptively strong landing gear and the dorsal fin.

Auster AOP 9 XS238, built to replace XP254 which became the Beagle-Auster AOP 11.

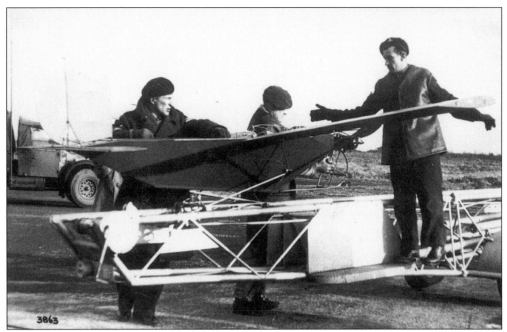

In the early 1950s Auster built 250 0Q3 radio-controlled target drones to an Air Ministry specification and contract. Here, one is prepared for launch by army personnel. Note the control vehicle in the background.

A target drone being launched from its mobile ramp. Powered by a small ABC petrol engine, it had a 6ft wingspan.

Three
Taylorcraft/Auster Aircraft Ltd (Civil)

One of only four Taylorcraft Auster 3s registered in the UK, G-ATAX (ex-RAF AOP III NJ916) initially went to Holland as PH-UFP. Restored in the UK during 1968 as G-ATAX, it also flew at the RAF Laarbruch Flying Club, Germany, where it is seen here. Ten years later it went to Australia to become VH-KRL.

Powered by a 90hp Blackburn Cirrus Minor 1, this Irish-registered Taylorcraft Plus C.2, EI-ALH, was initially G-AHLJ on the British register.

Taylorcraft Plus D G-AHXE, registered as such on 18 October 1946 (ex-RAF LB312).

Taylorcraft Plus D G-AHGZ, seen on 12 July 1952 at Woolsington where, piloted by Cyril Gregory, it won the King's Cup Air Race at an average speed of 113.5mph.

One of only four UK-registered Auster 3s, G-AHLK (ex-RAF NJ889) was used by Vickers (Aviation) until 1958. Sold to J.W.C. Judge, it was acquired by H.W. Bonner in 1969 and by F.W. Shaw & Sons (Worthing) Ltd in 1972, all at Shoreham.

This Auster 3 was converted in the Netherlands and entered on their civil register as PH-POL. It was one of a number of military machines disposed of by the RAF to the Netherlands and refurbished there for private use.

A Malaysian-registered Auster 3, VR-RBN, with a 130hp DH Gipsy Major Engine. This was one of some ninety civil Austers sold abroad, either as conversions or new for export, in the 1950s and early 1960s.

Many Auster AOP IVs, with 130hp Lycoming 0-290-3 engines, became civil Mk 4s. This one, G-AJXX (ex-RAF MT104), went to French Morocco in March 1952 and became F-DAAK.

The military Auster V included blind-flying equipment and was powered by a 130hp Lycoming 0-290-3. After the war many became civil Mk 5s, like this one, G-AJXC (ex-RAF TJ343).

This civil Auster 5, G-ANHO (ex-RAF MT169), was to crash at Biggin Hill on 9 May 1964.

Denham Air Advertising's Auster 5, G-AJVV (ex-RAF TW478), which crashed at Denham on 18 September 1952.

This Auster 5 was G-AIPE in the UK (ex-RAF TJ347) before going to Holland in June 1952 as PH-NET.

A smartly painted cowling for the 130hp Lycoming of Auster 5 3A-MAC, a Monaco registration.

Auster 5s were found far and wide. This is VR-SDY of the Royal Singapore Flying Club in the1960s.

Belonging here to the Yeadon Aero Club, Auster 5 G-ANID (ex-RAF TW471) unfortunately crashed near Oxford on 13 February 1958.

This Auster 5 (ex-RAF TJ 547) was sold to a French buyer in 1952 as F-BGPQ. On returning to the UK it was fitted with a DH Gipsy Major and re-registered G-AJLE, as shown here in 1984.

Auster 5 conversions included a number which had their Lycoming engines replaced by a DH Gipsy Major, retained the J/1N's vertical tail surfaces and became 5Ds. This 5D, G-AOCR, had five owners from 1956 to 1969.

With a DH Gipsy Major, a flat windscreen and enlarged fin and rudder, Auster 5D G-ANHX was at Southend from 1963 to 1969 and belonged to the Rochford Hundred Flying Group.

Powered by the 130hp DH Gipsy Major 1, this Auster 5D was registered in Hong Kong as VR-HFB.

This Auster 5D, G-AGLK (ex-RAF AOP V), flew with the Royal Artillery Aero Club, Middle Wallop, from November 1958 until 1967.

The enlarged rear canopy is apparent on this 5D, Irish-registered EI-AJS (ex-RAF NJ673/civil G-AOCR), seen inside its hanger.

Limited production of fourteen new Auster 5s as a purely civil type, without the enlarged AOP rear canopy, resulted in the Lycoming-engined Alpha 5. Here, Alpha 5 G-APAF is seen in 1967.

Auster Alpha 5 G-APBW, with its 130hp Lycoming. The plane was first registered in June 1957 by J.E. Allcard of Croyden.

To encourage the post-war light aeroplane market , a less powerful version of the Auster 5 was designed with a 100hp Blackburn Cirrus Minor 2 engine. Known as the Auster J/1 Autocrat, it proved very popular and over 400 had been built by the end of 1947. Here, early production Autocrats are under construction at Rearsby. Sixth in line, next to G-AGXB, is an export machine, OY-DGE, destined for Denmark.

Auster J/1 Autocrat G-AHHK in around 1967. The engine cowling side panels have been removed for inspection or maintenance of its 100hp Blackburn Cirrus Minor 2 engine. This machine was first entered onto the British civil register on 19 June 1946.

Many J/1 Autocrats were exported new or sold abroad second-hand. Here EI-AMK of the Irish Aero Club (ex-G-AGTV) carries racing number 19 in 1967.

Built as a direct export machine for Sweden, this colourful J/1 Autocrat, SE-ARL, has the 120hp Lycoming 0-235-C1 engine installed.

This J/1 Autocrat, G-AGTX , with the 100hp Blackburn Cirrus Minor, was first registered in December 1945 and remained in the UK until withdrawn in 1965.

Some Autocrats became J/1N Alphas, with a 120hp DH Gipsy Major and enlarged fin and rudder (to compensate for the longer nose). This J/1N Alpha, G-APCY, went to Britten-Norman Ltd in 1957 and to Nigeria in 1959 as VR-NDQ/ 5N-ACX. It returned to the UK in 1962, when it was restored at Farnborough. After going to the Airlines Flying Club, as seen here in 1966, it was sold to a private owner at Grimsby in 1968.

A New Zealand-registered Auster J/1N Alpha, ZK-BWH.

This Auster J/1N Alpha found its way to Australia where it was registered VH-SHS. Overseas customers could buy kits to convert a J/1 to J/1N configuration. The kits contained new fins and rudders, engine mounts and cowlings. DH Gipsy Major engines were available commercially and propellors could be obtained to order.

Originally a J/1 Autocrat, G-AGXT was converted to J/1N Alpha configuration in 1966 with Derby Aviation. It crashed at Birkmarsh in June 1969.

After converting from J/1 profile, Auster J/1N Alpha G-AHAL has been prepared for agricultural crop-dusting duties. Dusting was carried out via the under-fuselage dispenser. For spraying liquid chemicals, agricultural Auster conversions had Britten-Norman rotary atomisers mounted on underwing pylons.

Another J/1 to J/1N Alpha conversion, G-AIFZ, first registered as an Autocrat in November 1946. The type's name, 'AUSTER ALPHA', is shown on the fin.

Similar to the Alpha, the J/1B Aiglet was primarily an agricultural crop-spraying aircraft. Forced by a wind-driven pump, insecticide was spread over crops via spraying apparatus strut-fitted beneath the wing. This was easily removable if the Aiglet was required for normal purposes. The second J/1B Aiglet was G-AJYR, seen here. In 1950 this machine, accompanied by the prototype (G-AJUW) and G-AJYT, flew 3,200 miles to the River Nile in 34 hours of flying time on a spraying contract. Within a month they had spread insecticide over an area of 17,000 acres.

Here, J/1B Aiglet G-AYJR is seen when in service with Aerial Spraying Contractors Ltd of Boston, Lincolnshire (a company truck appears in the background). This Aiglet crashed while spraying in July 1964.

Auster J/1B Aiglet G-AMIH *Lady Lady*, in racing form (No.27). As such it came second in the Daily Express air race at Shoreham on 22 September 1951, piloted by T.W. Hayhow and averaging 135.5mph.

Registered here to Fison-Airwork Ltd at Bourn in 1958, J/1B Aiglet G-AMKU was with Pest Control Ltd from 1951 to 1953. It then went to the Sudan as SN-ABD/ST-ABD before returning to the UK. After two years with G.A. Barlow at Redhill it went to the Southdown Flying Group, Sussex, in 1964.

A more advanced agricultural J/1N update, the J/1U Workmaster had a 180hp Lycoming engine, the J/5R wing, J/5F ailerons, a dorsal fin and a 100-imperial-gallon tank for insecticides. The prototype (G-APKP) was built for Crop Culture (Aerial) Ltd for use in the UK, Sudan and Central Africa. Here G-APMH, the second of ten J/1Us built, is fitted with pylon-mounted Micronair atomisers, two each side, beneath the main-plane. Sent to SINCMA in 1959 as F-OBOA, it ended up with the Cornish Gliding and Flying Club, Perranporth, in 1970.

Here, J/1U Workmaster G-APSR (ex-F-OBHR) is in service with Crop Culture (Aerial) Ltd in 1959. It was sold to a Jamaican buyer in 1961 as VP-JCD.

The French-registered J/1U Workmaster F-OBOB in service with SINCMA in 1959. It was originally registered as G-APMI at Bembridge, UK, with Crop Culture (Aerial) Ltd. The Workmaster incorporated a strengthened J/1 airframe and gave valuable service as an agricultural aircraft in several overseas countries.

J/1U Workmaster G-APMJ with Cumberland Aviation Services Ltd, Silloth, in 1960. Sadly, it crashed near Loch Enoch, Kirkcudbrightshire, in October 1963.

Built for export, this J/1U Workmaster had the French registration F-OBRZ and operated in Mali on agricultural duties.

A production run of forty-four Auster J/2 Arrow side-by-side two-seaters began in 1946, but only a few sold in the UK. Powered by a 75hp Continental C-75-12 flat-four engine, most were sold abroad, including quite a number in Australia. This Australian-registered J/2 Arrow, VH-BDE, was christened *The Privateer*. It originated as Auster Aircraft's G-AIGW before export to Australia and was later destined for conversion to J/4 Archer configuration as VH-KFB.

One of the few British-registered J/2 Arrows, G-AJAM, which flew regularly with flying clubs around London for over ten years. It was first registered in March 1947 and was at one time with Wheels & Wings Ltd of Elmdon. The flat-four cylinder layout of its 75hp Continental engine is apparent here.

This Auster J/2 Arrow, sold in Belgium, carries the registration OO-ABU. The fuselage longerons are particularly prominent in this picture, as is the bluntness of the nose, which housed an American 75 hp Continental C-75-12 flat-four-cylinder engine.

This Auster J/2 Arrow, F/BAVS/'43', with a 75hp Continental engine and mass-balanced rudder, obviously joined the French racing circuits. It originated as G-AICA (previously Z-1 – the prototype J/2 of 1946), moving to France in October 1950.

With its 75hp Continental C-75-12 engine and mass-balanced rudder, this Auster J/2 Arrow found its way on to the Danish civil register as OY-ABY.

To overcome import restrictions on American engines, Auster installed a 90hp Blackburn Cirrus Minor 1 in the airframe of the J/2 Arrow, which thus became the J/4. Side-by-side twin seating remained and no flaps were fitted. However, the J/4 was not as popular as the three-seat Autocrat and only twenty-seven were produced, many ending up abroad. In Australia they were named Archer, like this one, VH-AAK (later VH-PJN), originally registered in 1947 as G-AIPJ of the Southend Municipal Flying School.

Auster J/4 G-AIJK which stayed in Britain from 1946 until 1968, when it was withdrawn. It flew with both Birmingham and Leicestershire Aero Clubs as well as two private owners.

With a smartly painted cowling covering its 90hp Cirrus Minor 1 engine, this Australian J/4 Archer, VH-CRR, has the name Archer on its fin.

This UK-based J/4 Archer, G-AIPR, at different times belonged to two private owners, the Heron Flying Group, Yeovilton, the Yorkshire Flying Club, Yeadon, and the M.P.M Flying group, Elstree, where it moved late in 1971.

The last J/4 built, G-APJM, in which major components from Auster J/2 G-APJU were used. It belonged to North Middlesex Flying group from 1959, but on 27 May 1961, crashed in the English Channel.

Called the Adventurer in Australia, the Auster J/5 was a J/1 Autocrat fitted with a small rudder and the 145hp DH Gipsy Major 1C. This one (VH-KAP) is seen in the 1950s operating with Rainair Taxi services.

Here, Auster J/5 VQ-CAB (ex-G-AMPV) is in service with Cyprus Airways Ltd, Nicosia, in the 1950s. It returned to the UK in 1960, entering service with Grantair Ltd, Sywell, but crash-landed at Ringway in June 1961.

With a domed cabin roof, wing-root fuel tanks and a 130hp DH Gipsy Major 1 engine, the four-seat J/5B Autocar first flew in August 1949. Seen here at that year's SBAC Farborough Show, the prototype, G-AJYK, retains a mass-balanced rudder, changed later to the familiar enlarged horn-balanced type. Most of the eighty-two J/5BS built were exported and some of the fifteen UK-registered machines were sold abroad later.

The eighteenth production J/5B Autocar, G-AJYV, in flight near White Waltham in 1952. Named *Bluesky* on the cowling cheat line, it was owned by I.M. Irkshire, but went to Spain in 1953 and became EC-AIR.

This Auster J/5B Autocar (G-AMFO) first belonged to Sissleys Cycles Ltd of Southend. It was sold to Huntings Aerosurveys Ltd but crashed in Scotland on 8 July 1955.

Built for export, Auster J/5B Autocar PH-NEH is shown here after delivery to the Netherlands. The legend 'Autocar' can be seen on the fin.

A 155hp Blackburn Cirrus Major 3 powered the J/5G Cirrus Autocar. This Australian machine, VH-ADX, was originally the British prototype J/5G, G-AMKG.

Three unsold export J/5Bs returned to the UK in the early 1960s to be refurbished at Rearsby by Beagle Auster Aircraft Ltd. One (G-ARLY) was a J/5P with a 145hp Gipsy Major 10 and the others (G-ARUG and G-ASFK), J/5Gs with 155hp Blackburn Cirrus Major 3s. Here, G-ARUG is smartly turned out with Beagle-designed wheel spats and colour scheme. It initially flew as G-25-9 to test a new glass/plastic wing covering.

The Auster J/5F Aiglet Trainer was not related to the J/1B Aiglet. J/5Fs had a slightly wider fuselage and shorter-span wings and were stressed for aerobatics. This is G-AMMS, the second J/5F, built in 1952 and powered by a 130hp Gipsy Major. It later became a J/5L, with a 145hp Gipsy Major 10 Mk2, and a year beyond that was converted to J/5K configuration with a 155hp Blackburn Cirrus Major 3.

This Auster J/5F Aiglet Trainer, G-ASLT (ex-Arab Legion Air Force A-409/OD-APB), owned by the Marquis of Headfort, was based at Biggin Hill during 1964.

Registered as G-ANSV, this J/5F Aiglet Trainer went to Barrow, Hepburn & Gale Ltd in 1954, passing later first to Luton Flying Club, then to Coventry (Civil) Aviation, Baginton. It crashed on 11 August 1965.

Auster J/5B Aiglet Trainer G-AMTB, which was at the Airways Aero Club of Croydon in the 1950s and went to Glamorgan Flying Club at Rhoose in 1963. In 1965 it moved to Mell-Air Ltd, where it stayed until withdrawn. It was sold for spares in 1968.

Registered D-EFEP in Germany between 1958 and 1960, this J/5F Aiglet Trainer was originally G-AMTC of the Airways Aero Club, Croydon. It returned to Coventry (Civil) Aviation Ltd.

A long way from home, this Auster J/5F Aiglet Trainer is in later-style Malaysian marking as 9M-ALF.

Originally registered in the UK as G-ANNW, this Auster J/5F Aiglet Trainer J-AAAE, with Kuwait Flying Club in the 1950s, was later re-registered as 9K-AAE. Note the added panels to help shield the tyres from the desert heat.

Powered by a 145hp DH Gipsy Major 10 Mk2 engine, the Irish-registered Auster J/5L Aiglet Trainer EI-ALN (ex-G-AOFS) arrived in Dublin during January 1960. It was refurbished in March 1961 and the following September went to Metnor Ltd of Woolsington. In June 1969 this aircraft was sold to G. Howard of Panshanger.

Prior to becoming EI-ALN in Ireland, J/5L Aiglet Trainer G-AOFS is shown here in its original British markings, some time between 1956 and 1959.

This Auster J5/L Aiglet Trainer, G-ANWX, powered by a 145hp DH Gipsy Major 10 Mk 2-1, was employed by Skyways Ltd at Lympne, Kent, from 1957 until the mid-1960s. A towing device can be seen below the tail unit The aircraft went to a private owner at Bicester in 1965 and was sold five years later to a lady owner on Teesside.

Auster J/5L Aiglet Trainer G-APVG of 1959. Intended as a J/5R Alpine for New Zealand, it was completed as a J/5L and went to the College of Aeronautics at Cranfield in 1961.

An updated version of the J/5B Autocar was produced for Kuwait Aero Club as the J/5P, fitted with a 145hp DH Gipsy Major 10 Mk2 engine. The first J/5P Autocar, G-ANXZ, built in 1955, was followed by some twenty others, a number of which remained on Britain's civil register. G-AOHF, shown here, flew with Gloster Aircraft Co. Ltd on communications work from around 1957 until 1962. After private ownership it went to Australia in 1970 and became VH-EDF.

Auster J/5P Autocar G-APKI was operated by the Dunlop Aviation Division at Baginton in the 1960s. Later, it crashed at Perranporth in May 1971 when owned by L. Phillips, its owner for a year.

Auster J/5P G-ARLY, seen operating with Bournemouth Air Taxi Co. at Hurn in the 1960s. Its appearance has been improved by adding wheel spats.

Caught on camera on one of Norway's fjords, this twin floatplane version of a J/5 series Autocar carries its Norwegian registration, LN-BWB. Interesting to note are the water-rudders on the floats.

Among a number of Auster J/5B Autocars directly sold for export in the 1950s was this one for Brazil, PT-ADL, in a rather smart finish.

This Auster J/5P, powered by a 145hp DH Gipsy Major 10 Mk1, was converted from a J/5B Autocar (G-AMNC) and sold in New Zealand as ZK-BVL to Mount Cook Air Service (as seen here).

Another improvement to the Auster layout emerged in 1960 as the J/5V Autocar, G-APUW, powered by a 160hp Lycoming 0-320-B2B engine. It was fitted with fibre-glass wheel spats, cuff fairings for the wing struts and a Workmaster tail unit. Employed as a development prototype for the Auster 'D' series, its main difference lay in having wooden main-spars as opposed to the metal ones seen in the 'D' type. G-APUW remained on the British register.

Sometimes referred to as an Auster J/1 Special, the Austalian-registered VH-AYJ originated in Britain as J/1 Autocrat G-AJPX during 1947. It went to Australia in 1951, where it was converted by Kingsford Smith Aviation ('Kingsmith' conversion) to accept a 150hp Lycoming 0-320-A1A (or A2A) engine. As can be seen, it was also updated by having wheel spats fitted, interior improvements and a smart paint scheme to boot. The mass-balanced rudder was retained on this variant.

The prototype for the Auster J/5R Alpine was this J/5L demonstrator, G-ANXC, fitted with Autocar wings and improved Aiglet Trainer ailerons.

Here, J/5L demonstrator G-ANXC, regarded as the prototype J/5R Alpine, is put through its paces at the 1955 SBAC Show piloted by Auster test pilot Ranald Porteous.

In addition to Autocar wings and an updated Aiglet Trainer aileron system, the six J/5R three-seater Alpines built had an Aiglet Trainer fuselage and empennage incorporated. Power was provided by a 145hp DH Gipsy Major 10 Mk 2 engine. All Alpines were built to special order including G-APAA, seen here in service with the Automobile Association in 1965, when employed on traffic surveillance duties.

Just four Auster J/5Q Alpines were built, two for the UK, one for Australia and one for New Zealand. They differed in having the lower-powered 130hp DH Gipsy Major 1 engine. This is the UK-registered G-AOZL, which went to two Elstree owners in succession, J.V. Heriz-Smith in March 1957 and Dr W. Zehden in October 1964.

The second UK-registered J/5Q Alpine, G-APCB, which was delivered to Jack Heywood Ltd of Yeadon at the end of June 1957.

This was the sole Auster J/5Q Alpine built as an export order for New Zealand, ZK-BLW. It appears to have a towing device at the rear end.

This one-off Auster J/8L, G-AMYI, was originally one of two J/5Ks produced, based on the J/5F Aiglet Trainer but powered by a 150hp Blackburn Cirrus Major 3. Here, in its J/8L configuration, it has been re-engined with a 145hp DH Gipsy Major 10 Mk2 and the cockpit has been experimentally fitted with a centrally located flap lever designed to be within the reach of both pilots. Its designation is stencilled on the fin.

Auster Mk 6 (ex-AOP 6 WJ370) G-APRO, the only one to be privately owned. It was converted for Air Commodore A.H. Wheeler at Old Warden in 1961.

Originally Royal Canadian Air Force (RCAF) AOP 6 No.16670, this civil Mk6 (CF-LWK) was converted in Canada. The half-span aerofoil flap was common to all Auster Mk 6s.

The prototype Auster 6A Tugmaster, G-ARCY (ex RAF AOP 6 TW624/7433M), converted by Auster Aircraft Ltd for glider-towing duties. Powered by a145hp DH Gipsy Major 10 Mk 1-1, it had an enlarged tail-unit with a horn-balanced rudder. Seating arrangements were revised, the pilot having an empty space to his right (where the radio had been in AOP 6) and the second occupant sitting behind in a sideways-facing seat. An electric winch and towing apparatus was mounted beneath the rear fuselage.

This Auster 6A tugmaster, G-ARGB, was originally AOP 6 VF635 with the RAF. In the 1960s, it served with the Three Counties Aero Club, Blackbushe, and Air Tows Ltd, Lasham.

Just touched down is Auster 6A Tugmaster G-ASNB (ex- RAF AOP 6 VX118), once of Air Tows Ltd, Lasham, and later in service with the West Wales Gliding Club in Haverfordwest.

A number of Auster 6A Tugmasters were sold abroad, like this one in Sweden, SE-ELF, which originated as AOP 6 TW571. The Beagle crest can be clearly seen on the fin.

A one-off ambulance/freighter design was produced by Auster in the early 1950s and designated the B.4. It featured a boxcar type of construction with a pod-and-boom layout, seating for four, rear-loading facilities and twin tail-wheels. Power was provided by a 180hp Blackburn Cirrus Bombardier 702 engine. Registered as G-AMKL, the B.4 was evaluated at the A&AEE, Boscombe Down, as XA177, but no orders were forthcoming for either a civil or a military version.

Auster's B.8 Agricola crop-spraying monoplane, like ZK-BMJ, shown here, sold well in New Zealand. Below and aft of the pilot, the aircraft was fitted with either a hopper, for carrying dry fertilizer, or a tank, for liquid spray.

The only Auster B.8 Agricola operated in the UK was G-APFZ. Here, it is in service with Aerial Agriculture Ltd at Lasham, fitted with a special tank and under-wing nozzles for crop-spraying. The B.8's engine was a 240hp Continental 0-470-B.

Rapid development of a four-seat executive tourer, the Auster C6 Atlantic, resulted in it being displayed at the 1957 SBAC Farnborough Show, fully furnished but minus its wings. Wider doors allowed easy access to front and rear seats, while a tricycle landing gear and 185hp Continental E-185-10 engine gave this design potential. It was test flown from Rearsby with a set of Autocar wings, but market research revealed sales of the Atlantic would be disappointing and it was decided the project should be abandoned.

Four

Beagle-Auster
After the Merger

Auster's later types were restyled Beagle-Auster after Beagle Aircraft's take-over in October 1960. Here, a two-seat D4/108 built for Portugal carries class B markings G-25-8 (it was later registered as CS-AME). The D4/108 first flew at Rearsby in February 1960.

The second two-seat Beagle-Auster D4/108, with the 108hp Lycoming 0-235-C1 engine. Carrying the Portuguese registration CS-AMA, it was displayed at the 1960 SBAC Farnborough Show.

This Beagle-Auster D5/160 (CS-ANE) was one of 150 licence-built in Portugal. It had an upgraded 160hp Lycoming 0-320-A2A and accommodated three people. The D5/160s have been used by the Portuguese Air Force as well as by civil flying clubs.

Initially delivered to Teheran, Persia, to assist with power-line installation in 1967, this Beagle-Auster D5/180 Husky (G-AVSR) returned to Britain in 1972. This version is fitted with a dorsal fin.

Powered by a 180hp Lycoming 0-360-A2A, this Beagle-Auster D5/180 Husky, G-ATMN, was owned by N.H. Jones of the Tiger Club and based at Redhill from March 1966. In July 1971 it passed to the Devon and Somerset Gliding Club at North Hill..

Originally delivered to Vienna as OE-DEW, this Beagle-Auster D5/180 Husky returned to the UK in October 1984 and became G-AXBF. It is seen here at a 'fly-in' during the summer of 1986.

Only three Beagle-Auster D6/180s were built, two of them British-registered. This one is G-ARDJ, on display at the 1960 SBAC Farnborough Show. A four-seater, the D6/180 had a 180hp Lycoming 0-360-A1A engine.

Many ex-RAF AOP 6 and T.7 Austers were converted for civil use as Beagle-Auster 6B/A.61 Terrier 1s. These had larger fins and rudders, improved ailerons and car-style upholstery. A 145hp DH Gipsy Major 10 Mk1-1 engine gave a cruising speed of 108-115mph. Terrier 1 G-ARXL (ex-RAF T.7 WE555) is seen here with the Three Counties Aero Club, Blackbushe, in the mid-1960s. It crashed on 16 May 1970.

Auster-Beagle A.61 Terrier 1 G-ARUX (ex-RAF T.7 WE611), which served with West London Aero Services Ltd until crash landing at Luton on 18 August 1963, when it was written off. Note the trailing exhaust system in which a lengthened exhaust pipe has been fitted with a silencer. This can be seen beneath the rear of the cabin.

Converted from AOP 6 VF581, this Beagle-Auster A.61 Terrier 1, G-ARSL (c/n 2539), made its first flight on 19 July 1961. A removed panel exposes part of its Gipsy Major 10 Mk1-1 engine.

The first production Terrier 2, G-ARLR, was a much-updated version which first flew on 25 April 1962. Features included interior soundproofing, fibreglass wheel spats, a ventral exhaust pipe and silencer, a Fairey-Reed metal propeller, an improved flap angle and a 2ft 7in increase in the tail-plane span. Many refurbished Terrier 1s were externally identical to the 2, having been fitted with an hydraulically damped tail-wheel spring.

Displayed at the 1962 SBAC Farnborough Show was the thirteenth production Beagle-Auster Terrier 2, G-ASBU. It was first registered to Beagle Aircraft Ltd, Rearsby, on 30 August 1962.

Distinguishable as a Terrier 2 by its hydraulically damped tail-wheel spring, D-ECKO was a direct export to West Germany (as it was then).

Originally Auster AOP 6 VW993, this A.61 Terrier 2 was registered in the UK as G-ASCD before being sold in Holland as PH-SFT (as seen here). It later returned to the UK and was restored in 1968.

This A.61 Terrier 2 ,G-ASMZ, was an ex-RAF AOP 6. Initially given the class B registration G-35-11, it has the 145hp DH Gipsy Major 10 Mk 1-1 engine.

A rebuilt AOP 6 (VW993), this A.61 Terrier 2, G-ASCD, first flew in this form on 18 September 1962. It is seen here in 1970, owned by Shackleton Aviation Ltd of Sywell.

Pictured in 1988, this A.61 Terrier 2, registered as G-ASAJ, is in Auster T.7 finish as WE569.

This aesthetically pleasing machine, A.61 Terrier 2 G-ASAN, was originally RAF Auster T.7 VX928. It was based at Kidlington from 1962 until 1964, when it was sold to R.G. Cooper at Blackbushe.

A hoist lift for Terrier 2 G-ASBU (ex-RAF T.7 WE570) after apparent failure of the starboard landing-gear strut. The engine cowling has been removed and the aerofoil flaps remain extended.

This Beagle-Auster A.61 Terrier was unique in being the only Terrier 3 ever built. It was completed by BEA apprentices at Heathrow, under the jurisdiction of Mr K.G. Wilkinson. The engine was a 160hp Lycoming 0-320-B flat-four as fitted to the Auster J-5V. Registered as G-AVYK, it was used during 1969 by the BEA/BOAC Gliding Club.

Built as an Auster AOP 9 replacement, the Beagle-Auster E.3 AOP 11 (XP254) was powered by a 260hp Rolls-Royce Continental 10-470D. After a first flight in August 1961, leading-edge slots improved its performance and the type showed promise. Sadly, an army decision to adopt helicopters for AOP work sounded its death knell and only one was produced.

Five

Beagle Aircraft Ltd
The Finale

Beagle-Auster became Beagle Aircraft Ltd in 1962 and this D5/180, G-ASBV, was a Beagle company demonstrator. It crashed in Belgium, was rebuilt at Rearsby and emerged as the first Beagle A.113 (D5/180) Husky. It is seen here at the 1963 Biggin Hill Air Fair fitted with balloon tyres, which enabled it to operate from rough terrain.

A much-refined Beagle version of the Auster was the A.109 Airedale, powered by a 180hp Lycoming engine. Features included a car-style cabin, wheel-type controls, swept fin and rudder, spatted tricycle landing gear and provision for all-weather flying instrumentation. This Airedale, G-ARXB, later went to the Five Star Flying Group.

Beagle A.109 Airedale G-ARNP, with a 180hp Lycoming 0-360-A1A, which went to Andrews Car Sales Ltd at Shoreham at the end of 1963.

Delivered on 29 May 1963, this Airedale, D-ENRU, went to Flugsport Club, Ebern (then in West Germany). It was returned to Beagle in January 1968 and registered G-AGWA, but was sold the following May to Irish Air Ltd as EI-ATA. It eventually returned to the UK, again as G-AGWA, being sold to Shackleton Aviation.

This Beagle A.109 Airedale OY-AOM, belonging to K. Jenson in Denmark, was first owned by British Executive Air Services at Kidlington as G-ASAF.

Beagle built five WA-116 gyrocopters for Wg Cdr K.H. Wallis, similar to this later Wallis WA-117 powered by a 100hp Rolls-Royce Continental 0-200-B.

The prototype Beagle 206 G-ARRM in landing mode. A five/seven-seat light transport, it had nose-wheel landing gear and two 260hp Continental 10-470A engines. It was Beagle's first major design and made its maiden flight at Shoreham on 15 August 1961.

Beagle 206 (Series 1) G-ATKP was built as a company demonstrator and charter aircraft. It had increased cabin space, wingspan, fuel capacity and tail area and was powered by two 310hp Rolls-Royce Continental engines. Seen here on lease to Air London at Gatwick, it passed to Shackleton Aviation before going to N.W. Velbo, Ostend, as OO-EEL.

After nearly a year's storage at Stollerton, this Beagle 206S (Series 2) – with two 340hp supercharged Rolls-Royce Continentals, a large freight door and extra cabin windows – went to Australia as VH-KCA with Groupair Ltd. It then passed in 1970 to Safari Air of Singapore as PK-OAS and helped support helicopter operations in Indonesia.

Beagle 206S G-AVGG, with special camera equipment internally fitted for a 1968 mapping expedition in Libya by Hunting Surveys Ltd. On its return to the UK in July 1968, it served as a company demonstrator, which included demonstrations for the Irish Air Corps and at that year's SBAC Show at Farnborough. It later went into storage, first at Shoreham and then at Biggin Hill.

Originally given the class B registration G-35-33, this Beagle 206S, G-AVHP, was delivered to the USA in July 1967 and became N966B on the U.S. civil register. It was later assessed by the Argentine Air Force at Cordoba, followed by a 1967 tour of South America. After being acquired by Air Carrier Inc. of Aerora, Oregon, this aircraft was later sold to J.P. Silberman of Savannah, Georgia.

A military version of the 206 was ordered for the RAF as the Basset CC Mk1 light communications aircraft. Here, XS769, delivered to Topcliffe in July 1965, is in contemporary RAF finish.

A nice aerial shot of Beagle Basset CC.1 XS771 of No.26 Squadron in 1971. Stored at 5 MU, Kemble, for two years, it went to 60 MU for disposal and was sold to Northern Air Taxis Ltd as G-BCJA.

An all-metal aerobatic monoplane designed by Beagle appeared in 1967 and was known as the Type 121 Pup. A two-seater, it combined American-style comfort with the handling qualities of British biplane trainers and was powered by a 100hp Rolls-Royce Continental. The prototype (G-AVDF) seen here first flew at Shoreham on 8 April 1968 and proved a winner.

Beagle Pup Series 1 G-AWEC, with 100hp Rolls-Royce Continental 0-200-A is seen here with the Shoreham School of Flying in 1968. It moved to Hong Kong in 1972 but retained its British markings.

The Beagle Pup Series 2 was a four-seater powered by a 150hp Lycoming 0-320-A2B. Originally registered G-AXFZ, this plane went to the Iraqi Flying Association in June 1969, becoming YI-AEL.

After the demise of Beagle in 1969, production of their successful Bulldog military trainer (a Pup development) was taken over by Scottish Aviation Ltd (SAL)at Prestwick. As well as serving with the RAF, Bulldogs flew with the air forces of Malaysia, Kenya, Ghana, Nigeria and Jordan. This Bulldog T.1 (XX517) is from the RAF Central Flying School in around 1974.

Beagle/SAL Bulldogs had a 200hp Lycoming 10-360-A1B6 engine. Here, Bulldog T.1 (XX707'04') wears the colours of Southampton University Air Squadron. The pilot's name below the cockpit reads 'Flt Lt K. Webster'.

This one-off Bulldog Series 200 (G-BDOG), with a retractable landing gear, a fourth seat and other refinements, is seen with Dukeries Aviation in 1980. It was later converted to the sole Bullfinch Series 2100.